EXTREME

Death Zone!

Can Humans Survive at 8,000 Metres?

Ross Piper

A&C Black • London

Produced for A & C Black by
Monkey Puzzle Media Ltd
The Rectory, Eyke, Woodbridge,
Suffolk IP12 2QW, UK

Published by A & C Black Publishers Limited
38 Soho Square, London W1D 3HB

First published 2008

ISBN 978-1-4081-0000-4 (hardback)
ISBN 978-1-4081-0071-4 (paperback)

Editor: Polly Goodman
Design: Mayer Media Ltd
Picture research: Lynda Lines
Series consultant: Jane Turner

This book is produced using paper that is made
from wood grown in managed, sustainable forests.
It is natural, renewable and recyclable. The logging
and manufacturing processes conform to the
environmental regulations of the country of origin.

Printed in China by C & C Offset Printing Co., Ltd

Picture acknowledgements
Corbis pp. 10 (Association Chantal Mauduit
Namaste/Sygma), 24 (Christophe Boisvieux); Film
and Mountain Ltd p. 29 (Brian Hall); FLPA pp. 5
(Colin Monteath/Minden Pictures), 6 Stefan Auth/
Imagebroker), 7 (Colin Monteath/Minden Pictures),
9 (Günter Lenz/Imagebroker), 11 (Colin Monteath/
Minden Pictures), 13 (Colin Monteath/Minden
Pictures); Johan Frankelius p. 4; Getty Images pp. 1
(David Trood), 8 (Time & Life Pictures), 15 (David
Trood), 16 left (PatitucciPhoto), 21 (Hulton Archive),
26 (Jake Norton); Nature Picture Library p. 23
(Asgeir Helgestad); Photolibrary.com pp. 16–17 (Uli
Wiesmeier/Imagestate), 27 (AlaskaStock); Reuters
p. 25 (Alexandra Beier); Rex Features pp. 12 (Sipa),
18 (Sipa), 19 (Suedtirolfoto/Helmuth Rier), 20 (Ms
Erin Copland), 22 (Aurora Photos); Ronald Grant
Archive p. 28 (Film Four/Pathe/UK Film Council);
Science Photo Library p. 14 (John Beatty).

The front cover shows a climber surrounded by fog
at the summit of a mountain in the Alps (PA Photos/
Uwe Lein/AP).

Every effort has been made to contact copyright
holders of material reproduced in this book. Any
omissions will be rectified in subsequent printings if
notice is given to the publishers.

CONTENTS

Abbreviations **m** stands for metres · **ft** stands for feet

Into the death zone

High up on the tallest mountains, there's a place where humans can't survive for more than a few hours. Mountaineers know this as the "death zone".

Climb up towards the freezing wilds of the death zone and you will start to feel sick and dizzy. Your head will begin to throb with piercing pain, you'll feel pins and needles in your fingers and toes, and you'll find it hard to breathe. You're suffering from **altitude** sickness, caused by a lack of **oxygen** in the air.

At 8,611 m (28,251 ft), K2 is the second-highest mountain in the world. Strong winds, ice and freezing temperatures make it a death trap.

Breathing practice

To avoid altitude sickness, before they climb into the death zone, mountaineers spend time at different altitudes to get used to breathing air with lower oxygen levels. This is called acclimatization.

On the summit of Mount Everest, at 8,848 m (29,028 ft), a mountaineer wears an oxygen mask to help him breathe. Everest is the highest mountain in the world.

altitude   the height of something above a certain level, for example sea level

The air at the top of a mountain is very different from the air at the bottom.

Death Zone

A third less oxygen in the air than at sea level.

7,600 m (25,000 ft)

Half the amount of oxygen in the air than at sea level.

5,000 m (16,000 ft)

Altitude sickness begins to affect people.

2,400 m (8,000 ft)

oxygen   a gas that makes up one-fifth of the air we breathe

The bare necessities

What things are important to you? Maybe your X-box? Or your football team? They might *seem* important – but there are some things that you *really* couldn't live without!

Humans need several basic things to survive:

- Oxygen: this is needed to burn up food for energy and to power the muscles.
- Drinking water: over half of our body is made up of water, and we need to keep it topped up to work properly.
- Warmth: to help keep our body at the temperature it works best at, which is 37 degrees Centigrade (98.4 degrees Fahrenheit).
- Food: for energy.

All these things are in short supply in the Death Zone!

In his tent, a mountaineer tucks into some dehydrated survival food that he has added water to. The food contains lots of energy.

Mountain menus

Mountain food has to contain lots of energy but weigh very little. Special dehydrated powdered meals are very light. Mountaineers just add water to them before heating. They take emergency rations in case things go wrong.

dehydrated   dried out by having water removed

6

Oxygen absorbed into blood from lungs.

Oxygen breathed into the lungs.

Oxygen carries nutrients around body.

Water and **nutrients** from food are absorbed into the blood from the stomach.

nutrients   substances in food that we need to survive and grow

Deadly weather

One day in May 1996, the death zone gave a terrible demonstration of its power. Eight people were killed in the worst accident in mountaineering history, and all because of the weather.

That morning, several groups of people had set out to climb Mount Everest. The weather was good and many of them reached the **summit**. As they stood at the top admiring the amazing view, however, a storm began to bubble up. The climbers rushed to descend as quickly as they could. Some of them were caught by the storm because they were too tired to move quickly. They froze to death.

This photo, taken on 1 May 1996, shows some of the climbers who were caught in a storm on Mount Everest on 10 May. This is the last photo of many of them.

When the wind changes

The weather can change very quickly on a mountain. This is because the higher up you go, there is less and less air. Higher up, the air is moved about very quickly, producing strong winds that push clouds around.

summit the highest point of a mountain

On a mountain, one minute there can be blazing sunshine, the next there can be a storm and a **whiteout**.

When clouds descend on snow-covered land there can be a whiteout.

In a whiteout, it can be difficult to see more than a metre in front of you. Climbers can easily lose their way.

High winds mean mountaineers cannot hear each other.

The mountaineers keep together by attaching themselves to a rope.

whiteout   when clouds and snow make it difficult to see

Shiver me timbers!

Cold can be deadly. Unfortunately, our bodies are not very good at adapting to it. That makes life even harder in the freezing temperatures of the death zone.

High in the mountains the cold affects you quickly. You get goose bumps as your skin tries to trap warm air in the fine hairs that cover your body. As your body temperature drops, muscles around your vital organs shake, to try and warm you up. This is shivering – the first stage of **hypothermia**. Eventually, if you don't warm up, you will die.

At night in the death zone, climbers sleep in all their clothes to fight off the cold.

Cold at the top!

- Air rising up a mountain drops an average 2 degrees Centigrade (36 degrees Fahrenheit) every 300 metres (1,000 feet) it rises.
- The temperature at the summit of Mount Everest can drop to -60 degrees Centigrade (-76 degrees Fahrenheit) in the winter. That's three times colder than a freezer!

hypothermia   when the body's temperature drops below the level that it can work properly at

The stages of hypothermia.

1. Blood vessels near the skin shrink to keep blood away from the cold surface.

2. Climber becomes pale and lips turn blue.

3. Breathing and heart rate slows as the body begins to shut down.

4. The brain shuts down and the climber becomes confused.

5. Death

Ouch! Cold that bites

Many mountaineers are missing a bit of a finger or a toe. Some have had to sacrifice a hand, a foot or even a nose to the mountains because they have been a victim of frostbite.

Frostbite happens if you stay in the cold for too long. Your extremities — the parts of your body furthest away from your heart like your hands, feet and nose — freeze. They turn black and the flesh dies. Body parts sometimes have to be **amputated** to stop the frostbite from spreading.

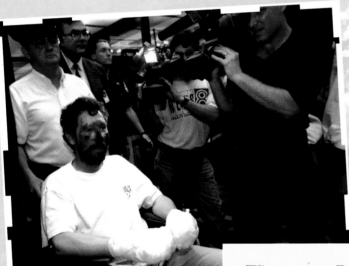

Beck Weathers almost died on Mount Everest. His face and hands were badly frostbitten.

Frostbitten survivor

Caught in a storm on Mount Everest in 1996, Beck Weathers spent over 18 hours up the mountain in sub-zero temperatures before regaining his senses and staggering back down. Both of his hands had to be amputated, but he was lucky to be alive.

frostbite   the freezing of part of the body when it is exposed to extreme cold

Andy Henderson was descending Mount Everest when he was caught in a bad storm. As the temperature dropped, he started to get frostbite in his fingers.

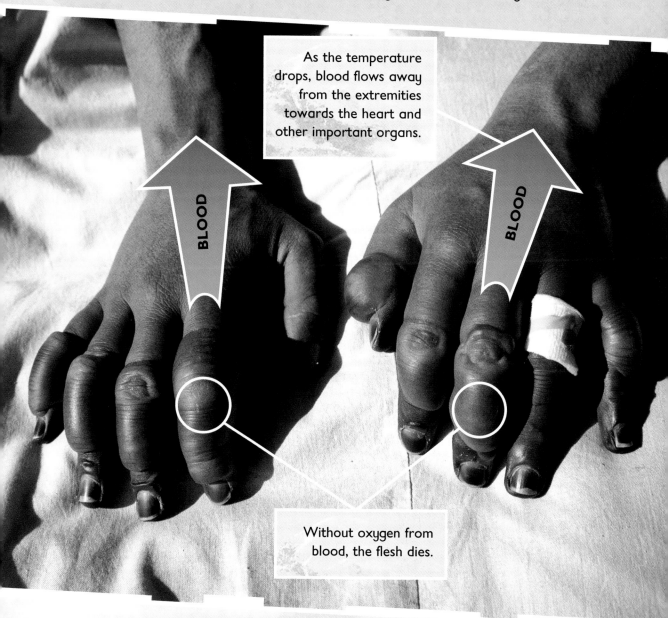

As the temperature drops, blood flows away from the extremities towards the heart and other important organs.

BLOOD

BLOOD

Without oxygen from blood, the flesh dies.

amputated   the removal of part of the body during an operation

Chilling winds

Imagine battling against gale-force winds while trying to keep your balance on a narrow ridge... That's what many mountaineers have to face in the death zone.

Chilled!

- A wind chill temperature below -50 degrees Centigrade (-58 degrees Fahrenheit) across your forehead would make you unconscious in minutes.
- A wind chill temperature of -75 degrees Centigrade (-103 degrees Fahrenheit) would freeze your skin in 30 seconds.

The wind can be deadly to mountaineers. **Jet streams** of fast-moving wind up to 500 kilometres per hour (310 miles per hour) can sometimes hit the tallest mountains. As well as the risk of being blown off the mountain, climbers have to watch out for wind chill. This is the loss of heat from skin exposed to the wind. The stronger the wind, the colder the air feels and the lower the wind chill temperature.

Mountaineers can measure the speed of the wind using a special device called an anemometer. It has several cups that are spun round by the wind, showing how hard it is blowing.

jet streams   fast streams of very high wind that circle the Earth

The wind at the top of a mountain is strong enough to blow you off your feet. These climbers are battling for every step.

Up to 40 per cent of the body's heat is lost through the head, so hats are essential for protection from wind chill.

Wind blows away warm air.

WIND

Body temperature **drops** as warm air is blown away.

Top gear

What do you pack to go on holiday? If you're going into the death zone, you'll need to take some really top gear to survive.

This mountaineer is using a Global Positioning System (GPS) device to help him find his location on a map.

Where am I?

Modern mountaineers use Global Positioning System (GPS) devices to help find their way. These devices, which are about the size of a mobile phone, calculate your exact position in the world using satellites.

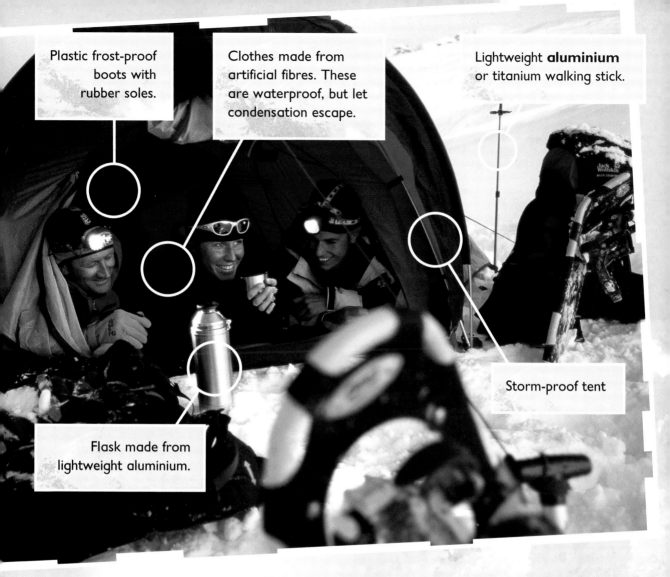

Plastic frost-proof boots with rubber soles.

Clothes made from artificial fibres. These are waterproof, but let condensation escape.

Lightweight **aluminium** or titanium walking stick.

Storm-proof tent

Flask made from lightweight aluminium.

These climbers are packed in tightly so that their body heat keeps them warm.

To survive in the mountains and reach the highest summits, you need lots of special equipment. Scientists have invented new materials to make clothes, ropes, tents and other equipment lighter and more waterproof for mountaineers.

aluminium   a lightweight silver-coloured metal that doesn't rust

Frozen in time

People have climbed mountains for thousands of years, but it must have been really tough in clothes made from animal skins.

In 1991, climbers in the Alps found the frozen body of a man in a **glacier**. Scientists worked out that he lived and died over 5,000 years ago. They think that he may have been injured by a hunter's arrow, then become weak from loss of blood and probably died from hypothermia. The man was nicknamed Ötzi the Iceman.

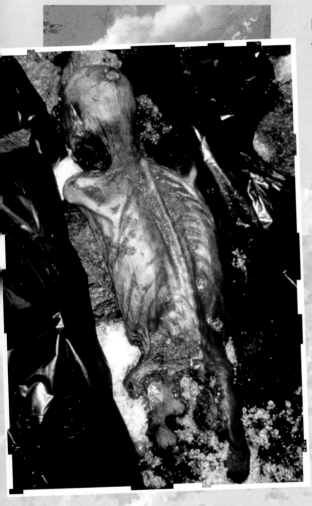

This is how Ötzi was found after being buried in a glacier for over 5,000 years. A pair of climbers found his body sticking out of the ice.

A 5,000-year-old snack

Amazingly, scientists have been able to identify what Ötzi ate before he died. They found he had two meals, one of mountain goat meat and the second of red deer meat, both with grain, roots and fruits.

glacier   a large, slow-moving river of ice

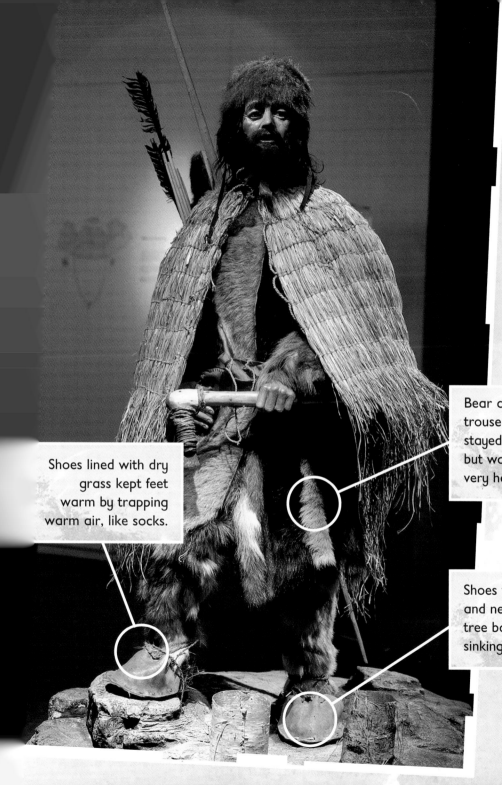

Ötzi's clothes were very different to the ones worn by mountaineers today. This model shows what Ötzi might have looked like when he was alive.

Bear and deerskin trousers and coat stayed dry in the snow but would have been very heavy to wear.

Shoes lined with dry grass kept feet warm by trapping warm air, like socks.

Shoes with wide soles and netting made from tree bark stopped Ötzi sinking in the snow.

A frozen body

Why would anyone want to climb a mountain? "Because it's there," was the reply of one of the world's most famous mountaineers – George Mallory.

George Mallory was one of the greatest climbers of his time. He disappeared while trying to climb Everest in 1924. Seventy-five years later, in 1999, his body was found over 8,000 metres (26,000 feet) up the mountain.

Carrying heavy equipment and wearing clothes that absorbed water, getting so high was a remarkable achievement. No one is sure whether Mallory died on the way up Everest or on the way down. He might have been the first person to reach the summit!

When Mallory's body was found in 1999, his skin was still on his body, bleached by the powerful rays of the Sun. His clothing and boots were also preserved.

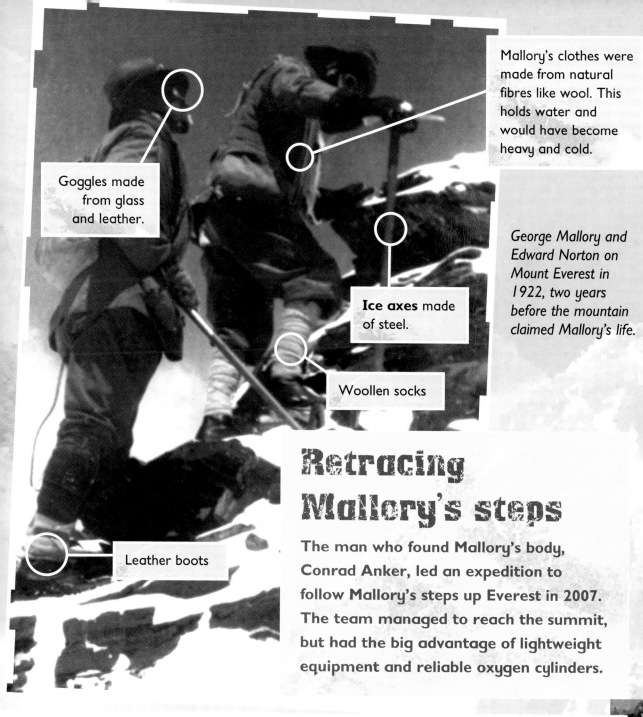

Goggles made from glass and leather.

Mallory's clothes were made from natural fibres like wool. This holds water and would have become heavy and cold.

George Mallory and Edward Norton on Mount Everest in 1922, two years before the mountain claimed Mallory's life.

Ice axes made of steel.

Woollen socks

Leather boots

Retracing Mallory's steps

The man who found Mallory's body, Conrad Anker, led an expedition to follow Mallory's steps up Everest in 2007. The team managed to reach the summit, but had the big advantage of lightweight equipment and reliable oxygen cylinders.

ice axes tools to help mountaineers climb on ice

Snow — friend or foe?

You're caught in a snowstorm and there's no shelter for miles around. What do you do? Dig a **snow hole**!

The tops of the world's tallest mountains are so cold that they have snow on them all year round. Snow can save a mountaineer stuck on a mountain. By digging a snow hole, mountaineers can shelter from the worst of the weather. This has helped many survive until rescue has arrived.

A mountaineer uses her shovel to hollow out the roof of a snow hole.

Snow words

The snowline is the height on a mountain above which there is snow all year round. Snowpack is snow and ice that has been on the ground for a long time.

A big snow hole can easily fit four people. Inside, they can cook, eat and shelter from the storm raging outside.

Body heat stays in hole.

Snow can be melted on a stove and used for cooking.

Ledges for cooking and sitting on.

snow hole   a shelter dug into the snow

Avalanche!

Imagine being submerged in tonnes of snow and plunged down a mountainside... One of the greatest fears for a mountaineer is getting caught in an avalanche.

Avalanches happen when lots of snow falls on an icy surface. If something disturbs the new snow, it slides off the ice and crashes down the mountain. Thousands of tonnes of snow and rock can fall down the slopes, wiping out everything in their path.

An avalanche crashes down Pumori mountain, near Mount Everest, in the Himalayas.

Getting out alive

If you are caught in an avalanche, try to "swim" in the snow to keep near the surface. As the avalanche settles, try to hold one arm up and keep a hand near your face. This will create an air pocket and allow you to breathe. Stay still to save energy and oxygen, and wait for help.

Rescue workers practise their avalanche rescue skills in Germany.

Long poles are used to find bodies beneath the snow.

Some mountaineers carry avalanche beacons that emit a radio "beep". Rescuers have radios that pick up the signals.

Special rescue dogs sniff out people under the snow.

Shovels dig through the deep snow.

Icy traps

Have you ever tried walking on an ice rink? It's very, very slippery! Imagine how difficult it can be walking up a mountain on ice.

Some mountains have glaciers spreading into their valleys. Glaciers move very slowly, over hundreds of years. As ice forms at the top it pushes the glacier down the valley.

Icy leaps

About 20 people die each year trying to cross crevasses in ice. Small crevasses can be jumped. Larger crevasses can be crossed using ladders.

As glaciers move, large cracks or **crevasses** open up. These can be very deep, and are sometimes hidden beneath snow. All it needs is a climber to put one foot wrong and they could fall in!

Mountaineers cross a crevasse using a ladder as a bridge. The ropes stop them falling down the crevasse if the bridge breaks.

crevasses   deep cracks or openings in the ice or snowpack

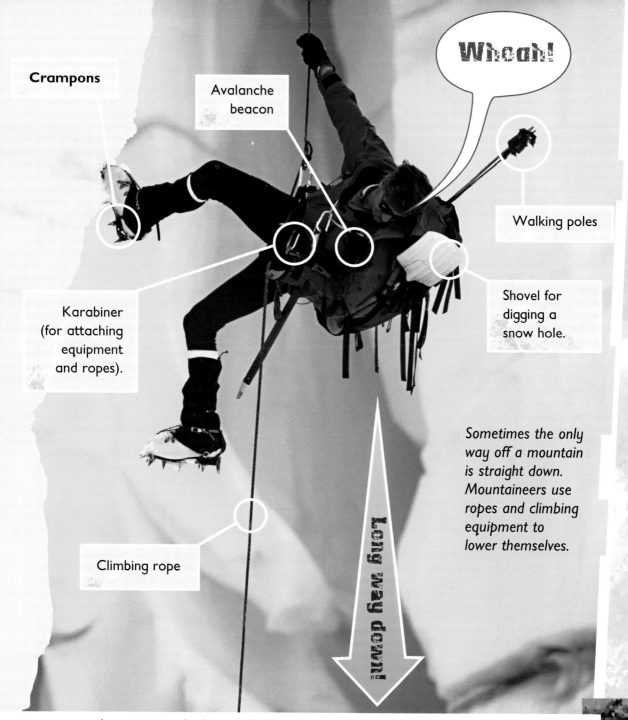

Crampons

Avalanche beacon

Wheah!

Walking poles

Karabiner (for attaching equipment and ropes).

Shovel for digging a snow hole.

Climbing rope

Long way down!

Sometimes the only way off a mountain is straight down. Mountaineers use ropes and climbing equipment to lower themselves.

crampons spikes worn on the boots of mountaineers and climbers to help grip

Against all odds

When things are against you, what makes you succeed? Using sheer determination, Joe Simpson survived an incredible ordeal.

The big screen

In 2003, Joe and Simon's amazing story was made into a film called *Touching the Void*.

In 1985, Simon Yates and Joe Simpson climbed the Siula Grande mountain in Peru. When Joe broke both his legs, Simon tried to lower him down the mountain using a rope, until Joe fell over an ice cliff. As Simon was dragged towards the edge of the cliff, he decided he had to cut the rope. Joe plunged into an icy crevasse, but against all odds he survived the fall.

*Joe managed to crawl out of the crevasse. He then spent three days getting back to **base camp**, navigating between crevasses as he dragged two broken legs behind him.*

base camp a safe place on a mountain used to reach the summit

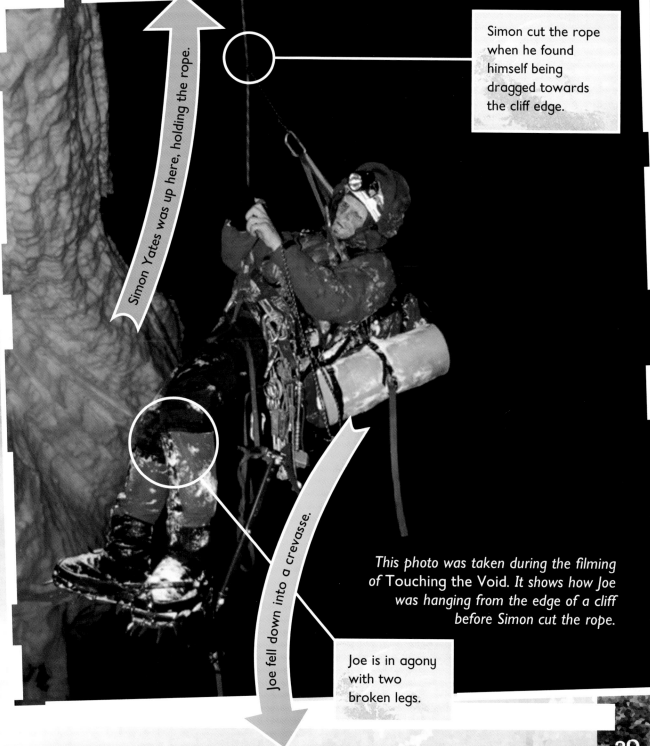

Simon cut the rope when he found himself being dragged towards the cliff edge.

Simon Yates was up here, holding the rope.

Joe fell down into a crevasse.

This photo was taken during the filming of Touching the Void. It shows how Joe was hanging from the edge of a cliff before Simon cut the rope.

Joe is in agony with two broken legs.

Glossary

altitude the height of something above a certain level, for example sea level

aluminium a lightweight silver-coloured metal that doesn't rust

amputated the removal of part of the body during an operation

base camp a safe place on a mountain used to reach the summit

crampons spikes worn on the boots of mountaineers and climbers to help grip

crevasses deep cracks or openings in the ice or snowpack

dehydrated dried out by having water removed

frostbite the freezing of part of the body when it is exposed to extreme cold

glacier a large, slow-moving river of ice

hypothermia when the body's temperature drops below the level that it can work properly at

ice axes tools to help mountaineers climb on ice

jet streams fast streams of very high wind that circle the Earth

nutrients substances in food that we need to survive and grow

oxygen a gas that makes up one-fifth of the air we breathe. It is the gas we need to stay alive

snow hole a shelter dug into the snow

summit the highest point of a mountain

whiteout when clouds and snow make it difficult to see

Further information

Books

Disaster in the Mountains!: Colby Coombs' Story of Survival by Tim O'Shei (Capstone Press, 2008)
Learn about how Colby Coombs used his wits and skills to survive in the mountains.

The Young Adventurers' Guide to Everest: From Avalanche to Zopkio by Jonathan Chester (Tricycle Press, 2005)
Find out about what to bring on a mountaineering expedition, how to handle frostbite, and much more.

Everest *(DK Eyewitness Books)* by Rebecca Stephens (Dorling Kindersley, 2001)
Lots of information on Everest and other mountains.

100 Things You Should Know About Weather by Clare Oliver (Miles Kelly Publishing Ltd, 2004)
Find out all about the weather in this book.

Websites

www.bbc.co.uk/sn/
The BBC science and nature website, with lots of information on the hows and whys of human survival in extreme situations.

www.bbc.co.uk/weather/ features/health_culture/ wind_chill_effects.shtml
The BBC weather website, including details about the effects of wind chill and other weather effects.

http://dsc.discovery.com/ convergence/survival/ guide/guide.html
The Discovery Channel Survival Zone website, including lots of information on extreme situations and how humans survive in them.

www.thesurvivalexpert. co.uk/SurvivingExtreme Heat.html
This website gives you lots of information on how you can survive in extreme situations.

www.ueverest.com
The website of the Altitude Everest Expedition, 2007, which followed Mallory's footsteps to the summit of Everest.

Films

Touching the Void directed by Kevin Macdonald (Pathé Films, 2003)
The incredible survival story of Joe Simpson and Simon Yates when they climbed the Siula Grande mountain in Peru (see pages 28–29).

Index